world vision
p u b l i s h i n g

PRINTED IN THE UNITED STATES OF AMERICA

Written & Compiled by:
Jeffrey Lawrence Benjamin
Michael B. Kitson
Thomas J. Powell

i

Book design by: Mike Kitson
Cover Design by: Alex Leutzinger, Gilbert Leiker & Annaliese Miller
Cover Photo: John Thomas Ravizé

World Vision Publishing, LLC
COPYRIGHT © 2003, World Vision Publishing, LLC
All rights reserved
Printed in the United States of America
03 02 01 00 99 12 11 10 9 8 7 6

Library of Congress Catalog Card Number: 200312302
ISBN 0-9727173-3-1

ii

world vision
p u b l i s h i n g

Also by these authors:

Real Life Habits for Success – Break Through Your Stress
Real Life Habits for Success – Master Your Communication
Real Life Habits for Success – Maximize Your Time

Special Thanks:

Cindie Geddes
Trace Geil

Dedication:

This book is dedicated to those people
who want to improve the quality of their lives.

FOREWORD

All it takes is one great idea, one little sentence, a simple concept, reinforced by action, to bring an abundance of prosperity and success into your life. This is the central idea of this book.

The ability to achieve is within each of us. Since we all possess a brain and a nervous system, it is possible to achieve our goals just as did Henry Ford, Leonardo da Vinci, Helen Keller, Amelia Earhart and countless others. If you're fed up with falling short of your heart's desires

or you simply want to improve your skills and achieve more, then this book may be the answer to obtaining the life you want and deserve. The driving purpose of these habits is to help you stay motivated, overcome challenges, break through barriers and achieve a higher quality of life.

Packed within these pages are simple and practical suggestions to help you improve your life. Invest a little time in reading this book, experiment with some of our suggestions and then watch as a world of opportunity opens up before you. You will find that your work, your

relationships and your sanity are all improved just by incorporating a few small changes into your thoughts and actions.

Best of success to you!

"When the occasion is piled high with difficulty, that's when we must rise to the occasion."

Abraham Lincoln

HABIT ~ 1

STEP OUTSIDE YOUR COMFORT ZONE ON A REGULAR BASIS

We like to do the same things over and over because we can predict the outcome; we can remain comfortable. However, attaining any worthwhile goal requires expanding your current comfort zone. The only way to expand that zone is by trying new things and stretching your boundaries. Make more sales calls in a single day than you've done previously, ask that person for a date, push yourself to exercise three-times-a-week, give a speech, attend a social engagement, introduce yourself to at least ten people at the next business mixer—whatever it is, step outside your box!

"My aspirations
have no bounds."

Mohandas Gandhi

HABIT ~ 2

EXPLORE YOUR PERFECT DAY ON PAPER

If you had a magic wand, what would you cast into your day? How about a brisk workout and massage in the morning and then a fun filled adventure with the family? Perhaps it's a day eating lunch with a good friend or reading a good book and relaxing after a busy day. How do you define your perfect day? Take five minutes to write down on paper what your perfect day consists of — how does it look, smell, taste, sound, feel? Give little or no thought to whether you can achieve your perfect day, simply script it out; it's quite possible the universe can deliver it to you. But you can't achieve it if you don't know what it is. Be creative, be specific, be bold, believe.

"Every adversity carries within it the seed of an equal or greater benefit."

Napoleon Hill

HABIT ~ 3

THINK IN TERMS OF OPPORTUNITY

Too many people are conquered by perceived negative experiences. But there is no such thing as a bad experience. Every experience we've had serves us for the betterment of our lives and well-being. People such as Oprah Winfrey, who were abused and who grew up in some pretty scary environments, were able to use their so called "awful experiences" to grow and excel. Often the adversities in our life are disguised as terrible misfortunes, when in hindsight they are our greatest opportunities. Always search for the good in seemingly negative experiences.

"Assume a virtue
if you have it not."

William Shakespeare

HABIT ~ 4

CHOOSE A ROLE MODEL AND IMAGINE YOU ARE THAT PERSON FOR ONE DAY

We learn to smile, walk and talk as a result of the people we model as we are growing through life. Once we see someone else do the seemingly impossible, a whole world of possibilities opens up. Roger Bannister was the first person to run a mile in less than four minutes. People were amazed a man could run so fast. It was only one month later that John Landy surpassed his record, and soon after many people were running the mile in under four minutes. Step into the shoes of the people you admire and respect and base your decisions on what they would choose to do. Let the achievements of others shape your vision for yourself.

"If you have enough whys,
you will most certainly
find a way how."

Friedrich Nietzsche

HABIT ~ 5

WRITE A LIST OF REASONS WHY YOU WANT TO ACHIEVE YOUR GOAL

Understanding the benefits you will receive from attaining your goal helps motivate you toward its fulfillment. To create the ongoing motivation that's needed to get you past the challenges you will face, you need to have strong reasons why you want to do what you want to do. The question is: What will you get once you have reached your goal? What types of new things will you be able to enjoy as a result of the work and effort you've put forth? What positive changes will you see in your life?

"If we all did the things we are capable of doing, we would literally astound ourselves."

Thomas Edison

HABIT ~ 6

REMOVE THE WORD "CAN'T" FROM YOUR VOCABULARY

As a general rule there is very little we can't do. When someone says, "I can't" they really mean they choose not to. If "can't" ruled the world we'd still be crawling on our hands and knees. And if we were able to walk, we'd be tripping on our shoelaces. Notice and correct times and areas in your life that you sell yourself short with a "can't" attitude. Search within yourself to find what part of you is saying "no." Uncover why you think you can't and then replace those thoughts with a "can-do" attitude!

"Courage is more exhilarating
than fear, and in the
long run it is easier."

Eleanor Roosevelt

HABIT ~ 7

DISCOVER WHAT FEARS ARE HOLDING YOU BACK

Fear is the killer of dreams, the grip of death! Research shows that we are born with only two fears: the fear of falling and the fear of loud noises. What that means is every other fear we have is learned. Unfortunately, we seem to acquire too many unhealthy fears that end up holding us back from living the life we deserve. It is essential to become more aware and to identify when we are fearful, how we respond to that fear, and how to break through it. Write a list of things you fear and then list ways you can overcome the fears that are holding you back.

"If you don't ask, you rarely get."

Jeffrey Lawrence Benjamin

HABIT ~ 8

CONSISTENTLY ASK FOR WHAT YOU WANT

The only way to get what you want out of life is by asking! This naturally begins at birth and follows us to the grave. As life progresses, it seems most people tend to lose the initiative to ask for what they want. The result is getting less than what they want. If you have fallen out of the habit of asking, start slowly. Make simple requests to remind yourself that you can and do get what you want, by asking. Is it going to work every time? Of course not, but will asking dramatically increase your probability of getting what you want? Yes!

"Do what you can, with what you have, where you are."

Theodore Roosevelt

HABIT ~ 9

OPERATE IN PRESENT-MOMENT AWARENESS

You've met people who are caught up in what happened in high school or those who live only for the notion of "someday..." Both your past and your future play a role in your life, but the leading role is the here-and-now! What you do right now, this instant, is what ultimately determines both your new history and your possible future. The key is to focus your energy on doing the right thing, right now; knowing the right result will follow.

"There are no mistakes,
no coincidences, all events
are blessings given to us to
learn from."

Elizabeth Kübler-Ross

HABIT ~ 10

DIRECT YOUR ENERGY
TO FIND A SOLUTION

Getting upset, yelling and screaming, or moaning and groaning, does little or no good. Too frequently people burn up all their energy complaining. Despite current difficulties it's in our best interest to be solution-focused. Let's face it, it's easy to find fault, blame someone else or dwell on a failure until is destroys us. The path less traveled is to immediately find a solution.

"You can't build a reputation on what you are going to do."

Henry Ford

HABIT ~ 11

ELICIT THE HELP OF OTHERS BY SHOWING YOUR COMMITMENT

Would you help someone if you thought that your time and energy would be wasted? If you want help from others, you must be prepared to show them, through action, that you are committed to doing whatever it takes to succeed. Multitudes of people will help you manifest your vision when they see you vigorously and persistently taking action. When you are valiantly committed to your purpose you will attract, like a powerful magnet, the people needed to make your dreams a reality.

"Bid me run and I will attempt things impossible."

William Shakespeare

HABIT ~ 12

BE CAREFUL NOT TO STIFLE OTHER PEOPLE'S GOALS AND AMBITIONS

Has anyone ever tried to smash your dream? How did that feel? When people voice their aspirations, give them words of encouragement. Avoid offering negative comments that trample on the enthusiasm and hopefulness of others. Far too many people have given up on their ambitions because they choose to accept the pessimistic opinions of people who did not believe in their pursuit. Get in the habit of supporting others by letting them know they can achieve anything when they apply themselves.

"Thousands of candles can be lighted from a single candle. Happiness never decreases by being shared."

Buddha

HABIT ~ 13

ESTABLISH A RELATIONSHIP WITH A MENTOR

People who are successful generally want others to succeed as well. It's extremely important to seek help from these people since we can learn from their experiences. You can accelerate your progress and avoid possible pitfalls to your eventual success. After you find a credible mentor, consult with your mentor on a regular basis. Make sure to report your activities and success to your mentor. Keep in mind that your mentor will continue to help you as long as you respect his or her time and knowledge, and you consistently progress toward your goals.

"You cannot help another person without simultaneously helping yourself."

Jeffrey Lawrence Benjamin

HABIT ~ 14

HELP OTHER PEOPLE ACHIEVE WHAT THEY WANT

The Law of Reciprocity basically states that what you get out of life is equal to what you give. By helping others you immediately begin to set in motion a universal law that will send you the help you need to achieve your goals as well. Give of your time and energy to help support the growth and achievement of others and you'll be brilliantly rewarded.

"Whatever you give your attention to, is the thing that governs your life."

Emmet Fox

HABIT ~ 15

POST YOUR GOALS WHERE YOU CAN VIEW THEM DAILY

We get out of life what we most think about. That's why it is crucial to post your goals where you can view them on a regular basis. It reminds you of what is really important to you in life. It is so easy to get caught up in the day-to-day distractions of life. One incredible way to focus your thought-power is to place your goals in your office on the wall, in your garage on large poster paper, or on 3x5 cards you can put in your car or in your calendar organizer. Reminding yourself of what you want is one of the best ways to get what you want.

"The best way to predict the future is to create it."

Erich Fromm

HABIT ~ 16

EXPERIENCE THE POWER OF YOUR WRITTEN GOALS

If it's not in writing it doesn't exist! Less than five percent of the population set goals in writing. Written goals produce better results than if goals are vaguely floating through your mind. Written goals are powerful roadmaps that can more easily lead you to the destination of your choice. Define what you want, in writing, giving thought and attention to all aspects of life such as health, business, relationship and recreational. Review them often!

"True success comes from maintaining your integrity."

Jeffrey Lawrence Benjamin

HABIT ~ 17

DO WHAT IT TAKES TO SUCCEED WITHOUT JEOPARDIZING YOUR INTEGRITY

No success is worth attaining if it requires that you surrender your innermost values and morals to get it. Keep in mind that if you end up jeopardizing your integrity, your success will be fleeting. Stand firm! You don't have to lie, cheat, trample or steal to get what you want out of life.

"One can never consent to creep when one feels the impulse to soar."

Helen Keller

HABIT ~ 18

REALIZE THAT A THOUSAND LITTLE "NO"S CAN LEAD TO A BIG "YES"

Rejection sucks, but that's no reason to give up. Rejection is part of life. It's a good thing Edison didn't give up when he was inventing the light bulb. It's been said that he tried 10,000 experiments before producing the incandescent light bulb. He then had to work hard to get the public to accept his invention. No matter where you are in life you have to learn to deal with rejection in a way that helps you take more action to get what you want. Let Edison's example illuminate your own tenacity.

"Make the most of yourself,
for that is all there is to you."

Ralph Waldo Emerson

HABIT ~ 19

ALWAYS BE ON THE LOOKOUT FOR WAYS TO IMPROVE

We'd still be cave dwellers if it weren't for the desire to improve living conditions. If you look at the most successful people and companies in the world you'll notice that they are tuned into a state of constant improvement. You can improve home or office efficiencies, or improve your communication, teamwork or leadership skills. Make a quick list of the things you want to improve and then take action to improve one item on the list within the next thirty days.

"You don't just luck into things as much as you'd like to think you do. You build step by step, whether it's friendships or opportunities."

Barbara Bush

HABIT ~ 20

DEDICATE ONE WEEK TO GIVING 100 PERCENT IN EVERY AREA OF YOUR LIFE

Take a one-week calendar and schedule your fitness time, family time, work time, spiritual time and leisure time. Strictly adhere to the allotted time schedule knowing you are giving attention to each area of life. Focus on giving all your attention and energy to each area during its scheduled time. In other words, don't spend time thinking of work when you are in a family time appointment. This is easier said than done, but it is possible for you. Prove it to yourself.

We make ourselves a ladder
out of our vices if we
trample the vices
themselves underfoot."

St. Augustine

HABIT ~ 21

CARRY FORWARD ONLY THE GOOD THAT COMES FROM PAST EXPERIENCES

Many people are so caught up in what happened yesterday that they have trouble moving forward today. That's like attempting to drive a car using only the rearview mirror! The majority of our decisions are based on past experiences. The trouble is that most people are accessing painful past experiences. To grow we must look for the good in our mistakes and misfortunes and learn from them so that we might make our today, and our future, brighter.

"The mind is its own place,
and in itself, can make a
heaven of hell,
and a hell of heaven."

John Milton

HABIT ~ 22

GIVE YOURSELF A REWARD UPON THE COMPLETION OF A GOAL

Images of enjoying a tropical vacation, relaxing over a romantic dinner, or buying a new car, house or boat may come to your mind when thinking of how to reward yourself after the discipline and effort you muster in the pursuit of your goal. Make a list of things you can reward yourself with as a result of your dedication and determination. You deserve the best, so why not work diligently in order to enjoy the many benefits you've earned.

"Who begins too much
accomplishes little."

German Proverb

HABIT ~ 23

ASK YOURSELF:
"WHAT CAN I DO IN FIVE MINUTES ?"

The way to eat an elephant is one bite at time. Search for small pockets of time you can use to accomplish your goals. Imagine what learning one new word each day would do to your vocabulary or how making one extra phone call per day would increase your sales. Break it down to the point of ridiculous. This will help to get the ball rolling and give you the momentum to keeping going.

"Habit is habit and not to be flung out the window by any man, but coaxed downstairs a step at a time."

Mark Twain

HABIT ~ 24

LIST POSITIVE ALTERNATIVES TO HABITS YOU WANT TO CHANGE

Make a list of some bad habits you want to extinguish and then make a list of new habits you want to acquire. Exchange your bad habit for a new more empowering habit. In others words, substitute a bad habit with a good habit. Instead of smoking, you'll go for a walk; instead of watching television, you'll read a book; instead of dominating a conversation, you'll listen. Your old bad habit won't go down without a fight so stick to your guns until the new habit settles in.

"The place to improve the world is first in one's own heart and head and hands and then works outward from there."

Robert M. Persig

HABIT ~ 25

EXAMINE WHAT SKILLS AND KNOWLEDGE YOU'LL NEED TO ACHIEVE YOUR GOAL

To expand physically, mentally and spiritually you need to acquire new knowledge and skills. Make a list of what you need to learn and resolve to take the classes, read the books and enter the mentoring relationships that will help you acquire the right knowledge and skill-set. No matter what you want to learn it's available on the Internet, in your local library or bookstore, or in a training program at work. Find out what you want to learn and then use all your resources to acquire what you want.

"Each person creates
the life they live by choosing
the words they speak."

Thomas J. Powell

HABIT ~ 26

STATE AFFIRMATIONS IN THE PRESENT TENSE

"I think I can...I think I can...I know I can..." Everyone remembers the Little Engine steaming its way to the top of the mountain. The story illustrates how affirming yourself in any given situation has a dramatic and powerful effect on what you can and can't do. When using an affirmation, remember to phrase it as if it were already true. Say, "I earn $75,000 a year," rather than, "I will earn $75,000 a year." Stating affirmations in the present tense allows you to become that person today, rather than someday.

"All that is needed to make a happy life is within yourself, in your way of thinking."

Marcus Aurelius

HABIT ~ 27

SCRIPT A FULL PAGE OF AFFIRMATIONS AND REVIEW IT OFTEN

What is your internal dialogue? Does it lift you up? Does it bring you down? Communication research shows that the average person carries on an internal dialogue at the rate of 500 to 600 words per minute. Unfortunately, most of that dialogue is negative. One incredible tool to interrupt negative thinking is to recall and silently recite affirmations. Write a list of affirmations and display it in a conspicuous place such as on your refrigerator, pinned up on your office or cubicle wall or taped to your bedroom door.

"Somewhere, over the rainbow, skies are blue. And the dreams that you dare to dream really do come true."

The Wizard of Oz

HABIT ~ 28

CREATE YOUR OWN MENTAL MOVIE

Become the director, the actor and the audience of your own movie. You can create a mental movie in which you see yourself eating less at meal times, see yourself taking smaller bites and chewing slowly, see yourself only eating wholesome foods. You can use a mental movie to create and reinforce any desired behavior. Play your movie over and over until your new behavior emerges.

"From a man's face I can read character; if I can see him walk, I know his thoughts."

Petronius

HABIT ~ 29

USE YOUR BODY TO CONTROL YOUR FRAME OF MIND

When you want to feel confident, you need to stand up straight, throw your shoulders back, breathe deeply and look slightly upward. The same is true if you want to be enthusiastic; simply adopt an excited and enthusiastic physiology. You can use your body to feel happy or sad, love or hate, energetic or lethargic. You have the power to feel any way you like simply by adopting the proper physiology.

"We lift ourselves by our thought; we climb upon our vision of ourselves."

Orison Swett Marden

HABIT ~ 30

WRITE A STATEMENT OF HOW YOU SEE YOURSELF

Who are you? Open your journal and write a brief statement of how you see yourself. Contemplate whether the image you have of yourself is one you want to enhance or overhaul. Make the necessary adjustments in how you see yourself to complement your goals and dreams. Take it a step further by projecting yourself five years from now and script how you would like to see yourself then.

"Above all things, reverence yourself."

Pythagoras

HABIT ~ 31

PRAISE YOURSELF UPON THE COMPLETION OF A GOAL

The most powerful reinforcement is self-reinforcement. Every time you do something that moves you in the direction you want to go, you have to reinforce that behavior. Give yourself a pat on the back or tell yourself what a great job you are doing. Big or small, whenever you do something right, praise yourself. For reinforcement to work, you must reinforce in the moment. Not before and not after, right then and there. You have dozens of successes throughout a given day, so remember to be good to yourself!

"Along the way, you learn not just what to do, but also what not to do."

Abraham Lincoln

HABIT ~ 32

BE PREPARED TO MAKE MISTAKES AND LEARN FROM THEM

If you expect to get it right the first time, every time, then you're in for a rude awakening. The key is to turn mistakes into magic! The only real mistake is repeating the same bad choices over and over. A mistake is really a learning opportunity. A large majority of the population is not willing to make mistakes, which generally results in fewer successes. Learn and adapt from your so-called "mistakes."

"The path to success begins when you ask what more can I give instead of what more can I take."

Thomas J. Powell

HABIT ~ 33

PRACTICE DESIRED BEHAVIOR
IN FRONT OF THE MIRROR

As children we become adults by mirroring our elders. Later, we daily dress and groom in front of a mirror to reflect back to us our appearance. If you have to speak publicly, for instance, would it help for you to rehearse what you have to say in front of a mirror before actually giving your presentation? Of course! Get in the habit of asking for a raise, asking for a date, talking with your children or rehearsing a business proposal in front of a mirror before actually doing it.

"In matters of style, swim with the current; in matters of principle, stand like a rock."

Thomas Jefferson

HABIT ~ 34

CEASE TO SEEK
THE APPROVAL OF OTHERS

Every extraordinary achievement is made possible by choosing to ignore the impossible. Trust yourself. Draw upon your own intuitive insights to guide you to your positive realization. Socrates, Galileo, Columbus, Edison and Einstein are appropriate examples of your power to manifest what you desire. Every great business, family and athletic champion has had to overcome what other people thought they were capable of achieving.

"When we cannot change a situation, resolution comes through the way we choose to handle it within ourselves."

Gerald Coffee

HABIT ~ 35

MAKE THE CHOICE TO WAKE UP HAPPY

No one but you can choose your destiny. You can certainly be influenced by outside sources, yet you have the ultimate power to interpret what positive perspective you adopt from your experiences. Resolve to be happy by making the necessary adjustments in your daily life. A good habit is to decide each night that you will wake up the next morning in an optimistic frame of mind. Follow this adage: search for the good and the good will appear.

"Do not let what you cannot
do interfere with
what you can do."

John Wooden

HABIT ~ 36

WRITE A LIST
OF YOUR POSITIVE QUALITIES

It's easy to forget what our strengths are if we focus on our weaknesses. Draft a list of your positive attributes. It's a good idea to get feedback from your friends, family and other associates. Review and savor your positive qualities. Refer to this list whenever you feel the need to get supercharged.

"Character building begins
in our infancy, and
continues until death."

Eleanor Roosevelt

HABIT ~ 37

DESCRIBE AN OBSTACLE THAT IS KEEPING YOU FROM YOUR GOAL

In football your goal is to score a touchdown, your obstacle is the other team. Professional sports teams study video footage of their opposing team in order to gain insight as to how to better overcome their obstacle. What potential challenges or obstacles stand between you and your goal, and what can you do to overcome them? Practice overcoming the obstacles in advance and then perform better, as a sports team does, when the real game is on.

"To keep a lamp burning we
have to keep putting oil in it."

Mother Teresa

HABIT ~ 38

HANG INSPIRATIONAL MESSAGES ON YOUR WALL TO KEEP YOUR MIND FOCUSED

Quotes, quips and other positive adages are wonderful reminders of successful living. The principles of teamwork, leadership and achievement can easily be introduced into your work or home environment by hanging inspirational messages on your walls. You can visit www.successories.com on the web to view and order portraits and other positive paraphernalia.

"You can't escape the responsibility of tomorrow by evading it today."

Abraham Lincoln

HABIT ~ 39

TACKLE CHALLENGES AS SOON AS THEY PRESENT THEMSELVES

A broken water valve can cause enormous damage if it's not attended to immediately. Running away from challenges will never make them disappear. Challenges are part of life and must be viewed as opportunities to learn and grow or life will surely offer only defeat. Keep in mind that challenges are like school yard bullies who end up shrinking when confronted.

"The crime which bankrupts men and nations is that turning aside from one's main purpose to serve a job here and there."

Ralph Waldo Emerson

HABIT ~ 40

INVOLVE YOURSELF IN THINGS THAT FULFILL YOU

The most successful people in the world are passionate about what they do. Figure out the types of things you enjoy doing and then do more of them. This may involve anything from describing your ideal career and taking the action to create it to rearranging your work schedule to spend more time with the family. Whatever it is, take more time to enjoy it.

"There can be no friendship
without confidence, and no
confidence without integrity."

Samuel Johnson

HABIT ~ 41

USE YOUR NAME AND YOUR WORD WISELY

Make yourself known as someone who gets things done, as someone to trust, as someone to rely upon, as someone with integrity. Too often people commit themselves and then end up not following through. This not only damages personal relationships, but also undermines personal confidence and self-esteem. The remedy: If you say you are going to do something—follow through!

"If you are what you do, then
if you don't, you aren't."

Dr. Wayne Dyer

HABIT ~ 42

KNOW WHAT IS IMPORTANT IN YOUR LIFE

If family is your top priority, but you are spending enormous amounts of time at the office, you may have a problem. Grab your journal or any piece of paper and list the three most important areas of life. Rank them in order of priority. Spend the most quality time on your number one priority.

"There are more pleasant
things to do than
beat up people."

Muhammad Ali

HABIT ~ 43

IDENTIFY WHAT GIVES YOU PLEASURE

As infants we are programmed to seek pleasure. Pleasure is a vital component of nurturing yourself and maintaining emotional balance. Make a list of the things that give you pleasure: talking with your best friend, listening to your favorite music, getting a massage, riding your bike, reading, socializing, making love, playing with the kids, watching movies, meditating, golfing or fishing. Keep your list nearby and engage in at least a couple of your pleasures every day.

"When down in the mouth,
think of Jonah, he came
out all right."

Thomas Edison

HABIT ~ 44

CHANGE YOUR FEARS INTO DESIRES

Focusing on what you desire instead of what you fear can be liberating. For example: Instead of "I'm afraid of not getting it right the first time," think "I'm going to learn and continue to get better." Or "I'm afraid I'll fail," can become "I have the chance to succeed." We generally experience whatever it is we focus on, so you might as well center your thoughts on what you desire.

"Self suggestion is the creator of character."

Napoleon Hill

HABIT - 45

USE THIS AFFIRMATION: "I TAKE ACTION NOW!"

Our behavior is controlled by our internal messages. Sometimes we get stuck and feel as though our feet are cemented in procrastination. When overwhelmed with procrastination, repeat: "I take action now," or "I do it now," or "Let's just get it over with right now." Remember you are in control of your mind as soon as you learn how to control your self-talk.

"Let us so live that when we come to die even the undertaker will be sorry."

Mark Twain

HABIT ~ 46

WRITE YOUR OWN PERSONAL OBITUARY

Taking the time to script your obituary can be revealing. Read through the obituaries in the paper to get in touch with what is being written about others. Most obituaries chronologically describe the life and achievements of the person. What would you like to see in your obituary? Use your imagination. Write your obituary describing your intended achievements and hallmarks of your life as if they had already occurred.

"All that is needed to make a happy life is within yourself, in your way of thinking."

Marcus Aurelius

HABIT ~ 47

FEEL THAT YOU ARE WORTHY OF HAPPINESS AND DESERVING OF SUCCESS

What's preventing most people from enjoying a bountiful life is that they feel unworthy; they feel undeserving. This decadent attitude breeds and slowly begins to deteriorate your chances of experiencing more happiness and success. A great exercise is to sit quietly and imagine that you are receiving your heart's desires. Note the feeling that is associated with the experience, and relive it often.

"Your daily habits
determine your destiny."

Jeffrey Lawrence Benjamin

HABIT ~ 48

MAKE A LIST OF DAILY POSITIVE HABITS YOU WANT TO DEVELOP

Do you want to drink plenty of water, floss your teeth, take evening walks, practice yoga, take vitamins or eat healthy meals? Whatever it is that you want to turn into a habit is possible through greater awareness. Write on a sheet of paper your list of daily habits you want to acquire. Keep this list on your desk or in your calendar organizer as a reminder of your new daily resolutions.

"Fear less, hope more, eat less, chew more, whine less, breathe more, talk less, say more, hate less, love more, and all good things will be yours."

Swedish Proverb

HABIT ~ 49

THINK OFTEN OF THOSE THINGS FOR WHICH YOU ARE GRATEFUL

Relish in all the blessings you enjoy. We have so many wonderful things for which to be grateful. The average person today lives better than the richest kings in history. So what are you grateful for?

"I not only use all
the brains I have,
but all that I can borrow."

Woodrow Wilson

HABIT ~ 50

EMULATE YOUR THREE GREATEST ROLE MODELS

From the cradle to the grave, we model the behavior of other people. We learn to smile, walk and talk by watching people. Most rock musicians became music lovers after seeing Elvis Presley or The Beatles. The key is to consciously choose people you would like to model. Write a list of people you admire or that you want to emulate. Choose the top three and begin to adopt the characteristics you admire.

"All truths are easy to understand once they are discovered; the point is to discover them."

Galileo Galilei

HABIT ~ 51

MAKE INTEGRITY THE CONERSTONE OF YOUR LIFE

Integrity is always doing the right thing, even when no one is looking. Integrity is when our actions are congruent with our values. Good friends of integrity are honor, truth, reliability, wholesomeness and honesty. Integrity is following through on what you say you are going to do and doing it right.

"Every thought you have, every word you say, every action you take plants a seed in yourself and into the universe."

Ian Hill

HABIT ~ 52

REPLACE NEGATIVE THOUGHTS WITH POSITIVE THOUGHTS

At times, negative thoughts seem to just jump into our brains. The way to combat negative thinking is positive thinking and positive action. Laugh at negativity when it shows its face. Think about your blessings, your successes, your goals and dreams. Use negativity as a cue to help you shift your focus to a more positive outlook.

"Go forth to meet the shadowy future, without fear."

Henry Wadsworth Longfellow

HABIT ~ 53

LEARN TO ENJOY UNCERTAINTY

People work dead-end jobs and stay in unproductive relationships because they are not sure of what to expect if they leave. Most people are so scared about uncertainly that they never act for fear they will make a mistake or fail. No great business leaders and relationship builders ever really know what to expect, but they are still willing to walk into the unknown.

"Many of life's failures are people who did not realize how close they were to success when they gave up."

Thomas Edison

HABIT ~ 54

PLAY THE NUMBERS GAME

Sales are down when the sales department isn't talking to enough prospects. When sales are down by 50 percent it would be a good idea to prospect twice as many people. If your manuscript is being rejected then send it to another publisher until it is accepted. Whatever it is that you want to achieve, keep on prospecting, swinging, shooting, practicing and playing—and you'll win.

"He who falls in love with himself will have no rivals."

Benjamin Franklin

HABIT ~ 55

AVOID ENGAGING IN SELF PUNISHMENT

Constantly beating yourself up over mistakes and misfortunes will destroy you. Telling yourself that you are no good or that you are not worthy or that you are stupid will only reinforce that type of behavior. If you didn't achieve a goal on time don't crack yourself over the head. Make the proper adjustments and move on.

"No matter how your heart
is grieving, if you keep believing,
the dream that you wish
will come true."

Cinderella

HABIT ~ 56

PLACE AN EMPOWERING BELIEF BEHIND EVERY GOAL

If you have a goal to get fit, but you believe exercise takes time away from your family, what is the probability you will exercise? Little to none! If you believe exercise means more quality time with family, you're more likely to exercise. When you believe something to be true, you literally behave in a manner consistent with that belief. The beauty is you can choose your beliefs. That's why Henry Ford said, "Think you can, think you can't; either way you'll be right."

"This became a credo of mine…attempt the impossible in order to improve your work."

Bette Davis

HABIT ~ 57

LIST THREE BELIEFS
THAT GIVE YOUR LIFE MEANING

In order for an Olympic athlete to win a Gold Medal she must first believe that she is going to win. Remember, you choose your beliefs. Brainstorm the types of beliefs successful people possess (or go ahead and ask some of your mentors). Maybe they believe that they have the resources to succeed at any undertaking or they believe that anything is possible when you think and act smart. Choose the top three empowering beliefs and begin to adopt them as your own.

"In the providence of the mind, what one believes to be true either is true or becomes true."

John Lilly

HABIT - 58

ELIMINATE DISEMPOWERING BELIEFS

Our beliefs tell us what is true and what is not true; what we are capable of, and what we are not capable of. People who believe that they are terrible at remembering names are terrible at remembering names. It's that simple. If you are not achieving what you want it is quite possible you are operating with a disempowering belief. You must comb through your mind and eliminate any belief that is not consistent with what you want to accomplish.

"Definiteness of purpose can, and should, so completely occupy the mind that one has no time or space in the mind for thoughts of failure."

Napoleon Hill

HABIT ~ 59

VISUALIZE THE ACHIEVEMENT OF YOUR GOALS

Every great achiever will testify that they saw their goal in their mind's eye before it was accomplished. Program your brain with visual imagery. Create a picture in your mind of you achieving the goal. Be specific. What does it look like? Who is there? What are you wearing? You can run your visual image before you retire at night or upon waking. The more you do it the higher the probability it will come true.

"We succeed only as we identify in life, or in war, or in anything else, a single overriding objective, and make all other considerations bend to that one objective."

Dwight Eisenhower

HABIT ~ 60

IDENTIFY WHAT YOU WOULD DO IF YOU KNEW YOU COULD NOT FAIL

If you could rub Aladdin's Lamp what wish would you ask for? If you could have anything, be anything or do anything, what would it be? If you knew you could not fail what would you succeed at? Contemplate your answers and begin to think about and take action on realizing your dream.

"Success is the ability to go from one failure to another with no loss of enthusiasm."

Winston Churchill

HABIT ~ 61

SHARE YOUR ENTHUSIASM

Enthusiasm is the fuel that ignites your soul and illuminates the lives of others. Throw a bucket of cold water on enthusiasm and it will turn to vapor before reaching its fire. People want to be associated with enthusiastic people because enthusiasm truly is contagious. It creates an energy and excitement that dissolves adversity and brightens everyday life. Share it freely.

"Happiness is that state of consciousness which proceeds from the achievement of one's values."

Ayn Rand

HABIT ~ 62

REVIEW AND PRIORITIZE YOUR VALUES

One of the greatest challenges people face in life is lack of value clarification. That is, they are unsure as to what is really important to them in life. A value is something you deem as important. A value is a belief about a concept's worth. Write a list of your top 10 values and then prioritize them in order of importance. Focus on being true to at least the top three.

"Life is what we make it,
always has been,
always will be."

Grandma Moses

HABIT ~ 63

REFUSE TO LET OBSTACLES KEEP YOU FROM YOUR GOALS

See obstacles and challenges as part of life and they will lose their power over you. Write out a list of obstacles that you might face when working on the completion of a goal. Next to the obstacle, write a few possible solutions to overcome it. Use these premeditated solutions when you come face-to-face with your dragon.

"Self pity is our worst enemy
and if we yield to it
we can never do
anything wise in this world."

Helen Keller

HABIT ~ 64

AVOID FEELING SORRY FOR YOURSELF

No one likes to come to a pity party. If you're engaging in a "poor me" attitude find a way to break your pattern. Read scripture, talk it out with a friend, listen to a motivational tape, review your gratitude list, consult a professional, watch a funny movie or help someone else in need. Just get out of the pity mindset and back to reality.

"Love yourself first and everything else falls into line. You really have to love yourself to get anything done in this world."

Lucille Ball

HABIT ~ 65

LEARN HOW TO LOVE YOURSELF

Society has adopted a negative belief that loving yourself means that you are conceited or arrogant. Nothing could be further from the truth. Those people who love themselves have the most to give. People who hold themselves in high esteem are the people who make the contributions that uplift the consciousness of the world. Whatever is impressed on the inside will be expressed on the outside.

"The best part of the future
is that it comes only
one day at a time."

Abraham Lincoln

HABIT ~ 66

BREAK GOALS INTO DAILY TASKS

The only way to climb a mountain is one step a time. Someday does not exist. Today is the only reality. Your life five years from today will be nothing more than the accumulation of all those days. And how you spend each one affects all others. Focus on breaking your goals down into manageable daily tasks. Use a calendar organizer to track the progress of your planning and tasking.

"The ideas I stand for are not mine. I borrowed them from Socrates. I swiped them from Chesterfield. I stole them from Jesus. And I put them in a book. If you don't like their rules, whose would you use?"

Dale Carnegie

HABIT ~ 67

TALK LESS AND LISTEN MORE

We learn by listening not talking. Remember the old saying: God gave us two ears and only one mouth so that we might listen twice as much as we speak. It's good advice. Learn from the mistakes and innovations of others and embrace the idea of a learning curve. A learning curve is necessary whenever we are moving toward a new goal. Listen to what people have done when they were in a similar position. Listen to your friends and business advisors about how to best pursue your goals and dreams.

"Success is having a flair for
the thing that you are doing;
knowing that is not enough,
you have got to work and have
a sense of purpose."

Margaret Thatcher

HABIT ~ 68

DO WHAT YOU LOVE

Successful people are successful because they fall in love with what they do or they do only that which they love. When you love your work it becomes a passion, not laborious. Many people go to work every day discontented, and their unhappiness starts to spread into other areas of their life. Uncover what lights your fire, what pumps you up, and resolve to turn it into a career. If that is simply not an option for you right now, find what is most rewarding or challenging in your current position and let it revitalize you.

"The secret of joy in work is contained in one word: excellence. To know how to do something well is to enjoy it."

Pearl Buck

HABIT ~ 69

ASK FOR AN APPRAISAL OF YOUR PERFORMANCE

Some companies carry out annual performance reviews. Leaders and achievers don't wait for a full year to go by before inquiring about their strengths and weaknesses. Ask your boss, your customers and your loved ones how you are doing. Ask them to be honest about what you do well and what you might improve. Avoid responding with any excuses, just listen and make the proper adjustments to increase your performance.

"To avoid criticism do
nothing, say nothing,
be nothing."

Elbert Hubbard

HABIT ~ 70

LEARN TO DEAL WITH CRITICISM

On your journey you'll undoubtedly encounter all kinds of criticism. People may say or write things about you that are not very pleasant to hear. Like water off a duck's back you'll need to find ways to effectively cope with criticism. If not, you'll drown in what people are thinking and saying. All accomplished people have had to endure criticism. If they're able to move past the negativity, then so can you!

"Television has proved that people will look at anything rather than each other."

Ann Landers

HABIT ~ 71

ELIMINATE TELEVISION AS A HABIT

Television can turn you into a couch potato and seemingly suck your brain right out of you. Four to five hours of television a day wastes valuable time that you could be spending on achieving your goals. This doesn't mean you should throw your TV in the garbage. Use it as an educational tool and as only a small part of your leisure time and recreational life.

"He who lets the world,
or his portion of it, choose his
plan of life for him, has no need
for any other faculty than the
ape-like one of imitation."

John Stuart Mill

HABIT ~ 72

WRITE AND MEMORIZE YOUR PERSONAL MISSION STATEMENT

Many successful companies, both large and small, use mission statements. Companies such as Federal Express, Ford Motor Company, J. C. Penney and Microsoft utilize the power of mission statements to direct their decisions and actions. Write a mission statement for your life. What is your personal credo or code of conduct? What is your long-term purpose? What kind of person do you want to be? How do you want to be remembered? Write it down and commit it to memory.

"Vitality shows not only in the ability to persist, but in the ability to start over."

F. Scott Fitzgerald

HABIT ~ 73

ALWAYS HAVE AN ALTERNATE PLAN

A back up plan can save your life, your career, even your sense of self. It demonstrates a willingness to persist if your original plan falls short. It shows you are persistent, flexible and grounded. Brainstorm and draft several viable plans that could potentially lead you to your goal. Choose what you believe to be the best plan. If for some reason it doesn't work, learn from your experience and move on to Plan B.

"That's one small step for
man, one giant
leap for mankind."

Neil Armstrong

HABIT ~ 74

KEEP AN EYE ON THE BIG PICTURE

Don't step over a dollar to pick up a dime. Base your decisions and actions on how they relate to the big picture. One example of big picture thinking is treating your customers right so they refer others and become customers for life. A good way to get a perspective on this is to ask yourself this question the next time you need to make a decision: "How will this decision affect my life one, five or ten years from now?"

"Nothing great will ever be achieved without great men, and men are great only if they are determined to be so."

Charles de Gaulle

HABIT ~ 75

DON'T REINVENT THE WHEEL

Most inventions are slight improvements upon previous products or ideas. Car manufacturers are notorious for making slight improvements to previous models every year. Pick up a book, jump on the Internet or grab paper and pen to record your findings. Research whatever it is you want to achieve and find models you can use—and improve upon.

"No man will make
a great leader who
wants to do it all himself."

Andrew Carnegie

HABIT ~ 76

DEVELOP A LIST OF PEOPLE
WHO CAN HELP YOU

No one climbs the ladder of success without the aid of someone else. Brainstorm on paper a list of people whose assistance and cooperation you want or need to achieve your goal. Choose the top ten names and write out how and why you want them to help you. Then write out how they might benefit from helping you.

"The outstanding leaders of every age are those who set up their own quotas and constantly achieve them."

Thomas J. Watson

HABIT ~ 77

SELECT THE RIGHT PARTNER

All sorts of chaos and challenges arise when we develop relationships with people we should not have been involved with in the first place. One of the biggest decisions you'll make in life is choosing the right partner: a person who does not stand between you and your goals but rather a person who supports you. It's a good idea to share your personal life and business career with people who have similar goals and values. Develop a list of qualities you'd like to see in your partner.

"Physical fitness sharpens
the mind and
strengthens the soul."

Jeffrey Lawrence Benjamin

HABIT ~ 78

ENGAGE IN PHYSICAL EXERCISE

If you've never begun an exercise program or fallen off your fitness schedule, now is the time to make your health a priority. Exercise provides you with the energy and stamina to keep moving forward when everyone else has lingered behind. It busts stress and releases brain chemicals that make you feel confident and optimistic. Choose from yoga, running, swimming, power walking, lifting weights, basketball, volleyball, racquetball—whatever suits you. Exercise at least three days a week and begin enjoying the benefits of an active life.

"It's kind of fun
to do the impossible."

Walt Disney

HABIT ~ 79

IGNORE PEOPLE
WHO SAY IT IS IMPOSSIBLE

Wilbur and Orville Wright decided to do what others thought impossible. Columbus was going to sail off the end of the earth. Flying in outer space used to be science fiction. The world is full of people who discourage possibility thinking. When someone tells you what you are doing is impossible use it to fuel your fire.

"You can achieve whatever you desire, but you must first define what you want."

Jeffrey Lawrence Benjamin

HABIT ~ 80

WRITE A CONTRACT WITH YOURSELF

Contracts hold agreements intact. Write a contract with yourself describing what you are willing to do in order to achieve your goal. What actions will you take, what behaviors will you engage in to achieve your goal and by when? Sign your name and add the date. Have a witness do the same. Give this contract to someone who will hold you accountable to following through.

"The price of greatness
is responsibility."

Winston Churchill

HABIT ~ 81

LIST YOUR ROLES AND RESPONSIBILITIES

You play many roles in your life, but what are they? Are you a mother or father, husband or wife, employee or employer, teacher or student? List the major roles you play in your life. Then list what your responsibilities are for each role. Determine to follow through on what you are responsible for. If not, get rid of the role.

"We are not responsible for the programming we receive as children; as adults, we are one-hundred percent responsible for correcting it."

Ken Keyes

HABIT ~ 82

BE ACCOUNTABLE FOR YOUR LIFE

There is only one person who can make you angry or happy—you. Only you can make your dreams and goals a reality because nobody is going to do it for you. Avoid getting caught up in blaming others for the state of your life. You attract your experiences by the choices you make.

"A flashlight with no batteries can't illuminate a dark room."

Jeffrey Lawrence Benjamin

HABIT ~ 83

REMOVE NEGATIVE PEO
FROM YOUR LIFE

Negative people can suck the life force right out of you. They require energy you could be using to take action on your goals. Spend little or no time with these people unless you are willing to go down like the Titanic. There are plenty of people out there in the world with whom you can develop optimistic relationships. Replace the ones that can't offer you any positive energy. Seek out positive people to be with and you will become more positive.

"If we are facing in the right direction, all we have to do is keep on walking."

Buddhist Proverb

HABIT ~ 84

REALIZE DELAYS ARE NOT NECESSARILY DENIALS

It would be nice if all of our goals were completed on time. Persevere. Perseverance is often the difference between success and failure. Many people give up when they are only steps away from their goal. You should always work vigilantly toward completions dates, but avoid wallowing in discouraging thoughts if the target date is not met. Evaluate your delay and then keep chipping away at the stone.

"Practice doesn't make perfect,
but whatever you practice at
can only improve."

Michael B. Kitson

HABIT ~ 85

THINK AND VERBALIZE ONLY POSITIVE THOUGHTS FOR AN ENTIRE DAY

This is the ultimate challenge. No matter what someone says or does or what event occurs during your day, think and verbalize only positive thoughts. When a negative thought crosses your mind transform it by thinking something positive. You can think about what you are most grateful for, think about your goals or think about a past successful experience. As soon as you are able to succeed at this all-important transformative exercise, repeat the process for another day. And another and another until a new habit is formed.

"…the gift of fantasy has meant more to me than my talent for absorbing positive knowledge."

Albert Einstein

HABIT ~ 86

WRITE A STORY IN WHICH YOU ARE THE HERO

Every great story has a hero, no matter the age, no matter the culture. You are the hero of your story. Use your imagination and write a short story with you featured as the hero. What obstacles will you face on your journey? What challenges will you defeat? What is your prize for moving forward and overcoming your adversity? Live the adventure, and then go live your life with the same purpose.

"The expectations of life
depend upon diligence;
the mechanic that would
perfect his work must first
sharpen his tools."

Confucius

HABIT ~ 87

ATTEND SEMINARS AND WORKSHOPS

Learn and practice skills that can lead you to the next level. Training programs in the field of personal growth and professional development enhance your awareness and skill level. Commit to practicing and improving your skill set every chance you get. Remember: The day you stop learning is the day you start dying. Learning is a life-long process!

"Time is the coin of your life. It is the only coin you have, and only you can determine how it will be spent. Be careful lest you let other people spend it for you."

Carl Sandburg

HABIT ~ 88

MAXIMIZE YOUR TIME

Each of us is created equal in that all of us are blessed with 24 hours a day, 60 minutes an hour and 60 seconds a minute. We all have the same amount of time in a given day. From Benjamin Franklin to Gandhi to Mother Teresa to Albert Einstein, right down to you—24 hours in a day! Consult Real Life Habits for Success: Maximize Your Time to learn more.

"Every human being has immense, incredible capacities of strength, of faith, of potential achievement. Become aware of them and use them."

Norman Vincent Peale

HABIT ~ 89

LOOK FOR THE GOOD IN EACH EXPERIENCE

Life for everyone is filled with challenges and opportunities. In each case it is important to state, "I can't wait to see the good that comes from this." This simple statement sets your brain in motion to look for the good in each and every situation. Remember that good always comes from tragedy, and people can still be disappointed during a celebration. The language you speak to yourself will allow you to always find the good.

"Only a man who knows what it is like
to be defeated can reach down
to the bottom of his soul and come up
with the extra ounce of power it takes to
win when the match is even."

Mohammed Ali

HABIT ~ 90

ALWAYS DELIVER MORE THAN EXPECTED

The team that wins the big game is often the one that practices past the point of exhaustion. The reason is the psyche learns to call on the hidden reserves of energy available to all, but called upon by few. A great way to increase your reserves is through physical exercise. Set a goal—say jogging for twenty-five minutes—and then periodically push past that goal, through exhaustion, for an additional 20 percent of time, distance or reps. Though it might seem physical, this habit is mental, and it can carry you through all challenges.

"Luck is what happens when preparation meets opportunity, and opportunity is always there."

Earl Nightingale

HABIT ~ 91

BE PREPARED TO SUCCEED

The toddler is prepared for kindergarten to be prepared for grade school to be prepared for college to be prepared for the work world. Most people stop preparing upon finishing their education. But that leaves two-thirds of a life yet to live. Don't lose out on opportunities because you simply don't see them. Leaders are readers and learners. Read, take classes, learn a new skill and be prepared for great things.

"America is the land of opportunity mostly because it applauds the achievements of the individual."

Thomas J. Powell

HABIT ~ 92

ALLOW FOR CREATIVE THINKING

Many great achievements have emerged from a single idea that something can be done to improve the current situation. The light bulb turned on for Edison well before he succeeded in the laboratory. Sit quietly each day and allow your brain to explore creative ideas that will improve not just your life but quite possibly the world in which you live.

"There is more to life than
increasing its speed."

Mohandas Gandhi

HABIT ~ 93

REWARD YOURSELF WITH RELAXATION

People are often so busy pursuing their goals that they neglect to nourish their bodies with rest and relaxation. Complete your list of goals with simple pleasures and think of them often. Use these pleasures as rewards for hard work. For more ideas consult Real Life Habits for Success: Break Through Your Stress.

"Did you ever observe to whom the accidents happen? Chances favor only the prepared mind."

Louis Pasteur

HABIT ~ 94

USE TIMELINES FOR YOUR GOALS AND ACTION STEPS

While developing your list of goals make sure to attach timelines for their achievement. Transfer your goals into action steps that can be placed onto your daily task list based on priority. Small steps taken over a period of time will lead to the achievement of huge goals.

"Write your life
to know your life."

John Kelly Eliason

HABIT ~ 95

WRITE YOUR AUTOBIOGRAPHY IN ADVANCE

Schedule time away from everything and everyone and outline your life from the perspective of living to 100 and looking back. Fill in your major accomplishments, the challenges you overcame, the people you touched. When you return, begin living the life you have designed with a roadmap to help guide you.

191

"A new idea is a light that illuminates presences which simply had no form for us before the light fell on them."

Susanne K. Langer

HABIT ~ 96

MAKE A RECORD OF YOUR IDEAS

Every day your brain processes ideas that can simplify your life. Each great invention started with an idea. The initial solution itself probably did not work but writing it down infused the idea with life. Ideas can change the world. Keep a small notebook with you and write down ideas as soon as they come to you. Write down any questions for which you need answers. Let your subconscious work out a solution through the pen.

"If you do your best, and always think and work positively, beautiful supply and abundant living will be yours."

Norman Vincent Peale

HABIT ~ 97

MASTER YOUR COMMUNICATION

Communication is vital for creating and maintaining effective relationships with family and friends. In the business world, your job requires you to get along with others so you can exchange ideas with coworkers and customers to achieve goals. And how well you communicate with yourself utimately determines who you are and what you can achieve. Consult Real Life Habits for Success: Master Your Communication to learn more.

"Forgiving others can bring freedom, peace of mind and a buoyant sense of lightness to those who learn to do it well."

Francine Prose

HABIT ~ 98

PRACTICE DAILY
THE ART OF FORGIVENESS

Eliminate all your enemies by forgiving them as soon as you realize you are holding in anger. Forgiveness is not for the benefit of the other person; it is for your physical and mental well-being. Forgive everyone, including yourself, and then forget about it!

"Any goal that is accomplished
alone is not big enough."

Thomas J. Powell

HABIT ~ 99

SHARE YOUR GOALS WITH OTHERS

Achieving the biggest goals in your life will require the involvement of others. Aggressive fitness goals are better met with help from a coach or personal trainer. Financial goals are best achieved when you seek advice from those who have earned what it is you seek. A strong marriage requires both people to prioritize the relationship. Rarely will you find a successful business that has only one employee or one client. Use this model in your life. Set big goals and then involve others to help you succeed.

"When you cease to make a contribution you begin to die."

Eleanor Roosevelt

HABIT ~ 100

MAKE A DIFFERENCE
EVERY DAY OF YOUR LIFE

In the movie It's a Wonderful Life, George Bailey is given the gift of seeing what a different world it would be if he had never been born. Is the world a better place because you have lived? Of course it is! Can you strive to make it even better to those that you touch in your daily travels? The answer is up to you. Whether it is passing on a smile, a compliment, spare change or finding the cure for cancer—living with an intent to improve the world makes it a better place for all those around you.

"A wise man will make more opportunities than he finds."

Francis Bacon

HABIT ~ 101

PRACTICE THINKING ON A DAILY BASIS

Every day opportunities pass in front of you. Two questions to ask yourself are; do you see the opportunity when it presents itself, and are you prepared to accept what the opportunity has to offer? For most people, opportunities pass them by because they are not prepared. The best way to be prepared is to THINK on a daily basis. To get started, read the book, Think and Grow Rich, by Napoleon Hill.

Write your own habits for achieving goals…

Achieve Your Goals

211

Jeffrey Benjamin

For more than 15 years author and speaker Jeffrey Benjamin has dedicated his life to passionately sharing career and personal achievement strategies with both small and large companies. He published his first book at the age of 23 and is the co-author of the acclaimed book series *Real Life Habits for Success*. He is also the host of his own television and radio show featuring leaders with real life success stories. Jeffrey is the founder of BREAKTHROUGH TRAINING, and a performance coach energizing thousands of people every month.

www.breakthroughtraining.com
toll free: 800.547.9868

Training & Coaching
Keynotes & Retreats

Mike Kitson

Mike is the founder and president of On-Call Graphics, Inc., a full-service creative studio in Reno, Nevada. OCG's mission is to work as a team, attract clients we enjoy, deliver uncompromising quality in a relaxing and creative environment. Mike holds his B.A. in Journalism from the University of Nevada. He has published over 20 books.

He is also the founder of the Forward Thinking Group, a group of consultants and coaches offering "Therapy for Business."

ON-CALL GRAPHICS | INC.
DESIGNING A BETTER IMAGE

www.oncallgraphics.com
toll free: 800.825.0448

Thomas J. Powell

Tom Powell is passionate about putting people into homes and helping them realize the American dream of homeownership. He is the President of *into*homes Mortgage Services LLC, one of the leading mortgage lenders in Nevada. He speaks regularly to business, educational and community groups on success, motivation and leadership. He attributes his own success to constant investment in personal and professional development, both for himself and his employees. He shares a home with his wife and four children.

intohomes MORTGAGE SERVICES   **toll free: 877-*into*homes**   ***into*homes**.com

J. T. and Lindé Ravizé have used their superlative photography and poetry to encourage legislators and the public towards exceptional stewardship of the natural environment. Their award winning work is being used extensively to support efforts to preserve Lake Tahoe, Big Sur, Wine Country, and other imperiled natural places.

Using their "Hearts of Light" book series, and museum shows around the country, they have reached a broad and enthusiastic audience and have become influential voices for the natural world.

Visit their website: www.aframeofmind.com
E-mail: jtr@aframeofmind.com
Or call their gallery "A Frame of Mind Gallery" 775-588-8081

Order Form

Please send me Achieve Your Goals for $8.95 per book plus shipping:

Quantity: $8.95 per book .... _____

Shipping: $2.00 per book .... _____

Total cost of book(s) and shipping cost: .... _____

For large quantity orders (10) books or more, please call 800.825.0448 for special discount pricing.

Full Name: _____

Mailing Address: _____

City: _____ State: _____ Zip: _____

MC/VISA/AMEX# _____ Exp._____

Check / Money Order for $_____ Payable to: World Vision Publishing, LLC

Daytime telephone number: ( ) _____

Signature: _____

Mail to: World Vision Publishing, P.O. Box 7332, Reno, Nevada, 89510.
Or call: 800.825.0448 to place your order today!